Brighten Up Boring Beginnings

and Other

Quick Writing Lessons

By Laura Robb

SCHOLASTIC
PROFESSIONAL BOOKS

NEW YORK • TORONTO • LONDON • AUCKLAND • SYDNEY
MEXICO CITY • NEW DELHI • HONG KONG

Thanks to all my students

who taught me well

and made this book possible.

Front cover and interior design by Kathy Massaro
Interior photographs by Bonnie Forstrum Jacobs

ISBN 0-439-07351-0

Contents

Introduction

Adults take as a basic assumption that writing communicates something *to* a reader and so is best if clear, specific, and exciting. Children, however, need to hear explicitly that the goal of their writing is to persuade, frighten, enchant, and so forth. In other words, our students need to be taught that writing, in a variety of ways, addresses an audience. This idea underlies the mini-lessons and writing warm-ups in this book; if your students understand that we write *for* readers, they will understand the goal of these exercises. Whether the aim of a lesson or activity is to find stronger verbs, enliven an introduction, or create an illustrative metaphor, the common purpose is to engage the reader.

I've included the mini-lessons and writing warm-up activities my students rate as top-notch for improving writing style and content. Since the mini-lessons and activities can each be completed in ten to fifteen minutes, they are ideal to use as warm-ups for writing workshop. They're also designed to be used as "Do Nows"—a quick, daily activity that challenges students to practice strategies and skills. In many school districts, teachers in grades 5 to 8 are now required to start a class period with this kind of activity. "Do Nows" can be written on the blackboard or a student activity sheet. Whatever you choose to call them, these activities are sure to build your students' understanding of writing.

Present a Mini-Lesson Before Each Activity

Mini-lessons are a powerful way to show students the inner workings of writing techniques. Before asking students to complete a writing activity, present a mini-lesson on the writing strategy or technique. Short and focused, these mini-lessons demonstrate how to revise writing with before-and-after models for students to study. REVISION TIPS suggest strategies for improving pieces.

Put the Ready-to-Use-Mini-Lesson Page on the Overhead

Each mini-lesson page in this book saves you valuable time, because it's ready for you to use. Make a transparency for an overhead projector. After presenting your mini-lesson, store the transparency in a file folder. Groups or individuals who need to revisit a mini-lesson can review the key points with the teacher or by themselves while the rest of the class completes another warm-up activity or works on a writing project.

You can use a water-soluble pen to write students' comments and suggestions on a transparency. With a damp tissue or paper towel, wipe off the comments and re-use the mini-lesson with small groups or individuals.

If your school does not have overhead projectors, write the mini-lesson on large chart paper. Review and revisit as needed.

Tips for Presenting Effective Mini-Lessons

Here are some suggestions that can strengthen your presentation of the mini-lessons:

1 Use a blank sheet of paper to cover up parts of the transparency you are not discussing.

2 Start by reading the title and the purpose.

3 Read the BEFORE EXAMPLE. Discuss it with students, asking them what they notice about the writing. Ask such questions as: Is anything repeated? Is any part confusing?

4 Read the revision tips. Discuss them with students, asking them if they have any suggestions for improving the BEFORE EXAMPLE.

5 Think aloud, pointing out what you believe needs revising.

6 Uncover the IDEA or BRAINSTORM BANK and the AFTER EXAMPLE. Read the revised example.

7 Stimulate discussion with the GET STUDENTS INVOLVED section. Use whatever time remains for students' input and questions.

8 Return to the GET STUDENTS INVOLVED section on another day if you have time for a fifteen-minute lesson. Ask small groups or pairs of students to rewrite the BEFORE EXAMPLE alone or with a partner. Compare completed work to the AFTER EXAMPLE on the transparency and invite students to offer reasons for the ones they feel are most effective.

9 After the mini-lesson, leave the transparency on the overhead. This way students can use tips, words, and phrases to guide their rewrites.

Tips for Evaluating The Activities

Here are some suggestions that can make each writing activity a valuable assessment and evaluation tool:

❋ It's not necessary to grade an activity. Read it quickly to see which students understood and internalized the mini-lesson and which students would benefit from repeating the mini-lesson and rewriting the activity.

❋ Students who need extra practice can complete the second activity that follows the main one. (These are labelled 1A, 2A, 3A, etc.)

❋ If students show they "get it" after completing the first activity, ask them to select a piece of writing from their folder to improve, applying the strategy or strategies they've practiced.

❋ You can organize peer helpers and pair students who understand the mini-lesson with those who need more practice.

❋ Once students can apply a writing strategy or technique, have them include it in their writing folders on a list titled "Things I Can Do." Students can review this list prior to editing a first draft and set individual goals.

PART 1

Improve Sentence Structure and Writing Style

When your students learn to pinpoint the following stylistic and organizational weaknesses, they will greatly improve their writing:

- Cluttering sentences with repeated phrases
- Telling readers what to think and how to feel
- Starting several consecutive sentences with the same word
- Jamming too many ideas into one sentence, thus forming a run-on sentence
- Using weak verbs such as *got* and *went*
- Including general nouns such as *flower*, *place*, *friend*
- Punctuating and setting up dialogue incorrectly
- Writing dialogue that reveals little about character and motivation

Section 1 spotlights these writing pitfalls, which are common in students' early drafts, and gives children practice in repairing them.

Brighten Up Boring Sentence Beginnings

Mini-Lesson 1

PURPOSE

to teach students how to revise paragraphs in which three to four sentences start with the same word

Before Example

I opened the door. I saw a cloud of black fleas greet me. I saw my dog trying to scratch himself with two legs. I saw fleas popping off his back. I ran outside to find my mom.

Revision Tips

1 Put a check next to sentences that all start the same way.

2 Rewrite. Try starting sentences with words or phrases from the Idea Box. Often, you can combine sentences or pull out a phrase that's in the middle of the sentence and use it at the beginning.

3 You might add or leave out some words of each sentence.

4 Read your revised paragraph and listen for the difference!

Idea Box

as soon as	suddenly	immediately	when	if
since	while	afterward	now	later
before	instead	unlike	yet	next
both	finally	meanwhile	after	as

After Example

I opened the door, and a cloud of black fleas greeted me. While trying to scratch himself with two legs, my dog whined. When I noticed puffs of fleas pop off his back, I ran outside to find my mom.

Get Students Involved

Ask: How did the AFTER EXAMPLE improve the paragraph? Are there other phrases or rewrites you like better?

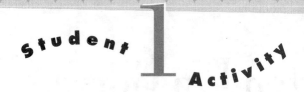

Directions: Rewrite the paragraphs below.

Activity 1

Rob's television remote control had magic powers. When he pressed the fast-forward button, his dog gobbled up the food and water in the red plastic dishes. When he pressed the rewind button, his dog vomited back all the food and water into the dishes. When he pressed the pause button, the dog froze and looked like a statue.

Rewrite: _____

_____

_____

_____

_____

_____

_____

Activity 1A

Every evening when Mike crawled into bed, he saw a spider's shadow on his pillow. Every evening Mike searched his room for the spider. Every evening he searched, he never found it.
One morning, Mike opened his eyes. A hairy black spider sat on his chest. The hairy spider walked towards Mike's face.

Rewrite: _____

_____

_____

_____

_____

_____

Combine Sentences for Smoother Prose

Mini-2
Lesson

Before Example

Jake and I walked to the park. We hiked through the wooded trail in the park to the lake. We rented canoes. We paddled the canoes around. Jake stood up in the canoe. The canoe tipped. We landed in the water. We tried to right the canoe. We couldn't turn the canoe over.

Revision Tips

1 Pinpoint repeated ideas that you can combine in one sentence.

2 Rewrite, eliminating unnecessary repetitions. Refer to the Idea Box for words and phrases that can help you vary sentence openings.

3 As you combine sentences, you might leave out or add some words.

4 Read your new paragraph to insure you've removed repetitions and varied sentence openers.

Idea Box

suddenly	several	every	finally	before
however	after	whenever	besides	soon

After Example

Jake and I walked to the park and hiked along the wooded trail that led to the lake. We rented canoes and paddled across the lake. Suddenly Jake stood up. The canoe tipped over, and we landed in the icy water. Every time we tried to right the canoe, it flipped over.

Get Students Involved

Ask: How did combining sentences improve the example? [no repetition; fluent; interesting, connects ideas that go together; more tension] Can you rewrite this paragraph another way? Which do you prefer and why?

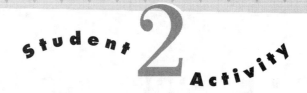

Directions: Rewrite the paragraphs, combining sentences to remove repetitions and choppiness.

Activity 2

The goblins and elves prepared for war. The war began when the goblins stole the elfin king's daughter. The war lasted many months. The goblins and elves fought their war in a meadow. The meadow was near the goblin's village. The meadow had a magic plant that put people to sleep for three months.

Rewrite: _____

_____

_____

_____

_____

_____

_____

Activity 2A

Our class took a trip to the zoo. The zoo was crowded with other classes. Maria and I lost our class. We were scared. We wondered how we would get home. We looked for our class in the reptile house. We looked for our class in the monkey house. We couldn't find our class. We sat on a bench and waited for someone to find us.

Rewrite: _____

_____

_____

_____

_____

_____

Don't Tell Everything, Show Your Readers

Mini-Lesson 3

PURPOSE

to change bland "telling" sentences that use overly general words into "showing" sentences full of specific, enlightening details

Before Example

My room is a mess.

Revision Tips

1 Brainstorm a mini-list of what a person might find in your bedroom to include in showing sentences.

2 Weave three to four ideas into one to two sentences.

Brainstorm Box

- broken cookies, popcorn, ants
- cards, board-game parts on floor
- sweaty socks
- homework

After Example

On patches of my room's wooden floor, tiny black ants feasted on chocolate cookie crumbs and stray pieces of buttered popcorn. A deck of cards and parts of board games teeter-tottered atop mounds of shorts, t-shirts, jeans, sneakers, and stiff, dirty socks.

Get Students Involved

Ask: Why is showing more effective than telling? [showing with specific details paints a picture for readers; engages readers by involving their five senses; allows reader to draw his own conclusions] Why is taking the time to brainstorm helpful? Can you rewrite this paragraph another way?

Student 3 Activity

Directions: Choose one telling sentence in each activity and rewrite it after you've brainstormed four to five ideas.

Activity 3

1 My sister/brother/cousin is a pain.
2 The pond feels slimy.

Rewrite: _____

_____

_____

_____

_____

_____

_____

Activity 3A

1 The store owner was mean.
2 The attic felt spooky.

Rewrite: _____

_____

_____

_____

_____

_____

_____

Use Transition Words to Improve Organization

Mini-Lesson 4

PURPOSE

to trade "ands," "then," "and thens" for transition words;
to use transition words to show order in time

Before Example

Sally wished that her stuffed duck was a real one and then it happened when she said the magic words she just learned. White downy feathers sprouted on her duck. Then the duck shook its webbed feet and quacked three times. Then it walked around the room.

Revision Tips

1 Read the story and circle all of the "ands," "thens," and "and thens."

2 Reread and place a check over the circled words you want to delete.

3 Find places where transition words could clarify the order of time.

4 Rewrite using transition words in the Idea Box to show the order of events. You might have to add or delete words and combine ideas.

Idea Box

before	after	now	previously	last
next	first	when	immediately	later
formerly	initially	presently	meanwhile	ultimately

After Example

The moment Sally mumbled magic words and wished her stuffed duck was real, something strange happened. First, downy white feathers sprouted on her duck. Then the duck shook its webbed feet, quacked three times, and walked around the room.

Get Students Involved

Ask: Besides adding transition words, what other techniques have been used in the AFTER EXAMPLE? [Ideas are linked; deleting the unnecessary conjunctions gives the sentences a more pleasing rhythm; the sequence of actions is clearer.] How could you organize the AFTER EXAMPLE differently?

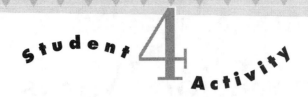

Student 4 Activity

Directions: Rewrite each paragraph.

Activity 4

Jimmy made his favorite sandwich for lunch. And then he took two pieces of whole wheat bread and put on peanut butter and then some grape jam. Then he cut thin slices of banana and cantaloupe and put a slice of bologna and a slice of liverwurst on top of the fruit. And he ate it.

Rewrite: _____

_____

_____

_____

_____

_____

Activity 4A

Maria baited her fishing hook with two juicy, squiggling worms and then she cast her line far out into the pond. Then she felt a tug on her line, and the float that was at the end of the line bobbed up and down and then went under the water. Maria reeled her line in, and as she turned the reel she saw a wriggling, whiskered catfish dangling from the hook.

Rewrite: _____

_____

_____

_____

_____

_____

Repair Run-on Sentences

> **PURPOSE**

to learn to spot and remedy run-on sentences

Before Examples

1 Evan caught a grasshopper he popped it into his mouth for a snack.

2 The caped stranger opened the secret door, walked up the stairs, and delivered the message to her chief and then when the sun had not set she decided to walk in the woods to hunt for lizards and spiders.

Revision Tips

Use these methods to fix sentence #1 and similar sentences:

1 Create complete sentences by adding periods and capital letters.

2 Add one of the connecting words from the IDEA BOX to create compound sentences. If you keep the subject in the second sentence, you will need a comma before the connecting word.

3 Separate two parts of a run-on with a semicolon(;), which takes the place of a period or a connecting word.

Use these methods to fix sentence #2 and similar sentences:

4 Rearrange sentences that are too long and contain ideas that don't relate to the main purpose of the sentence.

5 Create two sentences out of one that switches ideas or changes time or place.

Idea Box

and	but	so	although	yet	while
as	when	since	before	or	; [semicolon]

After Examples

Here are four ways to rewrite sentence #1:

1 Create two complete sentences:
Evan caught a grasshopper. He popped it into his mouth for a snack.

2 Add a connecting word, and remove the subject of the second sentence:
Evan caught a grasshopper and popped it into his mouth for a snack.

3 Add a connecting word and a comma, and keep the subject of the second sentence:
Evan caught a grasshopper, and he popped it into his mouth for a snack.

4 Use a semicolon instead of a connecting word:
Evan caught a grasshopper; he popped it into his mouth for a snack.

Here is one way to rewrite sentence #2:

The caped stranger opened the secret door, walked up the stairs, and delivered the message to her chief. Before the sun set, she walked into the woods and hunted for lizards and spiders.

Get Students Involved

Ask: Can you explain what can cause a run-on sentence? How can you locate run-ons in your own writing? Why do run-ons confuse readers? [Run-on sentences extend beyond three lines; include unrelated ideas; contain too many ideas; have two independent sentences without a conjunction or semicolon to connect them; switch from one place or one time to another.]

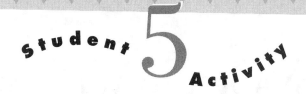

Activity 5

Rewrite the sentence three different ways.

1 The team met at an ice-cream parlor after the game they scarfed down hamburgers and ice-cream sodas.

Rewrite: _____

_____

_____

Rewrite: _____

_____

_____

Rewrite: _____

_____

_____

Activity 5A

Repair the run-on using any strategies you've learned.

1 Shantell climbed the steps to the high diving board she went slowly and looked like she was thinking about something serious she was because nobody knew that she couldn't swim.

Rewrite: _____

_____

_____

Activity 5B

Rewrite and repair the shifts in time and place.

1 Ricky met Josh at the mall in the morning to play games at the new arcade and in the evening the boys sold raffle tickets at their school's fund-raiser for the football team.

Rewrite: _____

_____

_____

_____

Wake Up Writing With Strong Verbs

PURPOSE

To replace weak, overused verbs with verbs that transmit the clear, colorful images in your mind

Before Examples

1 The boy *went* across the room toward the tray of chocolates.
2 Sheila *goes* to her grandmother's house after school.
3 Our starving girl-scout troop *went* to the cafeteria.
4 Phillipa *told* her friend the secret; her friend beamed after hearing it.

Revision Tips

1 Underline the verbs.
2 Brainstorm a mini-list of strong verbs that might be more effective.
3 Choose the verb that best expresses your ideas and creates a powerful mental image.

Brainstorm Box

- **went:** stomped, trudged, skipped, crept, slithered, hurried, charged
- **goes:** walks, rides, visits, pedals
- **told:** blurted, whispered, spilled, confided

After Examples

1 The boy *crept* across the room toward the tray of chocolates.
2 Sheila *pedals* her bike to her grandmother's house after school.
3 Our starving girl-scout troop *charged* into the cafeteria.
4 Phillipa *whispered* the secret to her friend; her friend *beamed* after hearing it.

Get Students Involved

Ask: How did your mental images change when you read the AFTER EXAMPLES? [Strong verbs create vivid images because they often carry other associations or meanings. For example, *crept* gives the boy's action a stealthy spin, as though he's a cat in pursuit of a fish bowl.] What other verbs would work? Why?

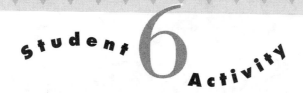

Directions: Replace each underlined verb with a strong verb.

Activity 6

1 The eagle <u>went</u> for a fish.

_____

2 The orchestra conductor <u>used</u> his baton

_____

3 Armondo <u>ate</u> the banana split and <u>said</u> it was delicious.

_____

4 After finding out she'd won the lottery, Pam <u>walked</u> across the living room and <u>told</u> her husband the news.

_____

5 Genna <u>went</u> into the deep end of the pool and <u>swam</u> quickly to the other side.

_____

Activity 6A

Tip: It's okay to rearrange and add words when you revise.

The race <u>began</u> and cheerleaders <u>said</u> a funny cheer. We <u>were</u> out of our seats because we <u>wanted</u> our runners to win. If we <u>got</u> this trophy, we would also <u>get</u> the district trophy.

Rewrite: _____

_____

_____

_____

_____

 Mini-Lesson 7

Switch From Passive to Active Verbs

Before Examples

1 Josh and his dad *were taken* to the Caribbean Islands in a sailboat.
2 The house *was destroyed* by a tornado.
3 The baby *was bitten* by a stray dog.

Revision Tips

1 Underline the verb in the passive voice.
2 Eliminate the helping verbs such as *am, is, are, was, were*.
3 Rearrange the words in the sentence to eliminate the helping verbs. You may have to change the main verb's ending.

Brainstorm Box

 were taken in a sailboat—sailed    was bitten—bit

 was destroyed—destroyed

After Examples

1 Josh and his dad *sailed* to the Caribbean Islands.
2 A tornado *destroyed* the house.
3 A stray dog *bit* the baby.

Get Students Involved

Ask: How does the active voice improve sentences? [It creates a sense of immediacy and energy; it clearly conveys the action described.] Why did you have to rearrange some words?

Directions: Rewrite, changing the underlined verbs to the active voice.
It's okay to rearrange and add words when you revise.

Activity 7

1 Two boys <u>were bitten</u> by a rabid dog.

_____

2 Angela <u>was told</u> by the magician that he could turn her into a rabbit.

_____

3 The experienced gymnast was <u>challenged</u> by a young opponent.

_____

4 Carlos <u>was ordered</u> not to ride his brother's bike.

_____

Activity 7A

Two earthlings, a man and a woman, <u>were taken</u> prisoner by alien soldiers. The pair <u>were pushed</u> down a long flight of steps and <u>were shoved</u> into a dungeon. For weeks they <u>were held</u> in the tiny cell and <u>were given</u> stale bread and water to eat. The aliens waited until the man and woman <u>were starved</u> enough to cooperate.

Rewrite: _____

_____

_____

_____

_____

_____

_____

Sharpen the Image With Specific Nouns

PURPOSE

to improve writing by changing general nouns to specific nouns

Before Examples

1 Gloria received different *things* for her birthday.

2 We played *games* for a long *time* on a rainy day.

Revision Tips

1 Underline general nouns such as *stuff*, *things*, *flowers*, *games*.

2 Brainstorm specific nouns to replace general words. Specific nouns are like snapshots: they enable others to imagine what you see.

3 Replace general words with the best specific nouns.

4 Rearrange, add, or delete words to improve the sentence.

Brainstorm Box

things: secret diary, a green sweater, running sneakers

games: Monopoly, checkers

time: a rainy afternoon, near midnight, sunrise, early spring

After Examples

1 For her birthday Gloria received a secret diary, a green pullover sweater, and high-top running sneakers.

2 On a rainy day we played Monopoly and checkers to pass the time.

Get Students Involved

How did specific nouns sharpen the images? Why are specific words more interesting than general words?

Directions: Choose three sentences and change the underlined general words to specific nouns.

Activity 8

1 At the grocery store, mom bought <u>lots</u> for dinner.

_____

2 Three lizards shape-shifted into <u>different things</u>.

_____

3 To build that dollhouse, she used <u>many materials</u>.

_____

4 Our club sponsored the dance and decorated the gym with <u>stuff</u>.

_____

Activity 8A

1 Mom and I went on a shopping spree and bought <u>everything</u>.

_____

2 Shaundra wanted <u>many things</u> for Christmas.

_____

3 The children played with <u>toys</u>.

_____

4 Our club sold <u>different dried foods</u> to raise money.

_____

Who's Talking?
Punctuating Dialogue
Lets You Know

PURPOSE

to teach that when the speaker changes, it's time to start a new paragraph; to demonstrate how to use quotation marks and punctuation in written dialogue; to show that no quotation marks are needed to signal a character's thoughts

Before Example

Ernesto opened his locker. No shorts, no shirt, no sneakers. Did you see anyone go into my locker Ernesto asked Carl. I just got here answered Carl. I didn't see anyone. I'll find him Ernesto mumbled as he walked around the locker room and spotted Jimmy combing his black hair. Those are my sneakers, my shorts, and shirt thought Ernesto. Where'd you get those gym clothes Ernesto asked Jimmy. From my locker sneered Jimmy. Well said Ernesto, I think... Why you asking? Jimmy interrupted. Ernesto looked at the dark scowl on Jimmy's face. He's wrestling champ, thought Ernesto. I guess I'll have to miss class today.

Revisions Tips

1 Read the story, and identify words such as *said, answered, replied, told, sneered*. These words tell you someone is speaking.

2 Find the speaker's words, and place a check over the first and last word the speaker says.

3 Place quotation marks around the speaker's words.

4 Insert punctuation before the closing quotation marks (, . ? !).

5 Don't place quotation marks around inner thoughts. Instead, use words such as *thought, wondered,* and *told herself* to indicate inner dialogue. Use a comma between the thought and the thinker (He's a wrestling champ, thought Ernesto).

6 Start a new paragraph when the speaker changes.

After Example

Ernesto opened his locker. No shorts, no shirt, no sneakers. "Did you see anyone go into my locker?" Ernesto asked Carl.

"I just got here," answered Carl. "I didn't see anyone."

"I'll find him," Ernesto mumbled as he walked around the locker room and spotted Jimmy combing his black hair. Those are my sneakers, my shorts, and my shirt, thought Ernesto. "Where'd you get those gym clothes?" Ernesto asked Jimmy.

"From my locker," sneered Jimmy.

"Well," said Ernesto, "I think—"

"Why you asking?" Jimmy interrupted.

Ernesto looked at the dark scowl on Jimmy's face. He's wrestling champ, thought Ernesto. Without gym clothes, I'll have to miss class today.

Get Students Involved

Ask: How does separating the speaker help you read the passage? Discuss the different kinds of punctuation placed before the closing quotation mark. Can you locate inner thoughts? How do these help you understand Ernesto?

Investigate How Authors Use Dialogue

Have students find a page of dialogue in their free-choice reading books and discuss the following questions: How does the author of your free-choice book punctuate the dialogue? Does the dialogue give you information about the characters, the setting, or the plot? Are there examples of inner thoughts? What do you learn from the inner thoughts?

Directions: Correctly rewrite the dialogue from this story.

Steven walked down the school bus aisle, looking for someone who did the math homework. He slid into the empty seat next to Charmayne. She's soft on me, thought Steven. That's what his best friend Jamal told him last week. How's it going? asked Steven. Fine answered Charmayne, looking straight ahead. Listen, said Steven. My little brother was so sick last night, and I was the babysitter and couldn't do any homework. I hope he's better Charmayne politely replied. Yeah, he's better. But if I don't have my math homework today, it's the principal's office for me. Could I copy yours, just this once he asked. I'm not sure. It's really cheating whispered Charmayne. Think of it as helping me, just this once, pleaded Steven. Just this once said Charmayne. And she opened her notebook.

Rewrite: _____

_____

_____

_____

_____

_____

_____

_____

_____

_____

_____

_____

_____

Write Introductions That Grab the Reader

In just a few sentences, the openings, or introductions, of stories and books can hook readers, making them wonder and question and turn page after page until they reach the end. Some introductions, however, have the opposite effect. They send signals that say, "boring, snoozer" and cause readers to shut their books.

In Part II, your students can practice four kinds of introductions that arouse curiosity and pull readers into writing. After students draft a piece of writing, ask them to think about and decide which kind of introduction will work best with their topic.

Revision Tips

1 Reread your piece. Think of unusual facts.

2 Use the BRAINSTORM BOX to jot down ideas.

3 Use the IDEA BOX to help you revise.

4 Pick the ideas that will make readers think, WOW! and read on.

5 Write two to three introductions using your best ideas. Playing with words and ideas helps you find unusual ways to start a piece of writing.

6 If you're writing an essay, make sure the last sentence of your introduction is a link to the next paragraph.

7 Ask a partner to read your rewrites, pick the one that worked best, and explain why.

8 Think about the purpose of your piece. For your final draft, think about your partner's suggestions. Then select the introduction that best supports your purpose.

Give Your Topic Sentence All You've Got

P U R P O S E

to create topic sentences that hook readers

Before Examples

1 I'm going to tell you about the mystery I read.
2 This report is about the preying mantis.
3 The Boston Tea Party was the cause of the American Revolution.
4 This summer we went camping in Canada.

Brainstorm Box

- Will a question be effective?
- What was unusual about Canada? (A visit from bear cub)
- What's fascinating to include about mantis—female eats mate.
- Boston Tea Party—colonists tossed 340 boxes of English tea into Boston Harbor

After Examples

1 This mystery was so gripping that I read it on the school bus, at recess, and at lunch.
2 When a female preying mantis is hungry, she pounces on and devours her mate.
3 Why did the American colonists disguise themselves as Indians and throw 340 chests of English tea into Boston Harbor?
4 The morning a bear cub poked its head into my tent, I wondered why we were vacationing in the Canadian wilderness.

Get Students Involved

Ask: Why is a topic sentence important? How did the BRAINSTORM BOX help? How would you start one of these sentences now? Discuss.

Directions: Choose two topic sentences to rewrite.

Activity 10

1 In-line skating is fun.

2 I'm going to tell you about my dog (cat, bird, hamster).

3 This was my worst (or best) birthday.

4 My favorite sport is _____.

Rewrites: _____

_____

_____

_____

_____

_____

_____

Activity 10A

1 _____ is the best season ever.

2 I'll never forget my performance in the school talent show.

3 This is about the time I got lost on a field trip.

4 My visit to my grandparents (or any friend or relative) was memorable.

Rewrites: _____

_____

_____

_____

_____

_____

Begin With An Unusual Fact

PURPOSE

to show students how to draw readers into a piece of writing with an unusual fact or event

Before Example

Earthworms have many enemies.

Brainstorm Box

List two to four interesting facts about earthworms, such as:

* moles attack underground
* people dig up for fishing
* box turtles bite worms in half after rain

After Example A

On a stormy day, pounding rains force earthworms out of their underground homes. Quickly, a hungry box turtle bites worm after squirming worm in half until there's enough for a feast. Worms have many enemies above ground.

After Example B

Earthworms squiggle and squirm on the wet meadow grass. A box turtle searching for dinner quickly bites worm after worm in half. Soon the turtle has enough worms for a tasty feast. Whether worms stay above or below the ground, they have many enemies.

Get Students Involved

Ask students: Which introduction did you like best? Why? Can you suggest another way to rewrite the BEFORE EXAMPLE?

Directions: For each activity below, choose a sentence to rewrite, brainstorm two to four unusual facts, and compose two new opening lines that make it irresistible for readers.

1 It was an embarrassing moment.
2 I like my pet [dog, cat, horse, fish, etc.].
3 My family is wacky.
4 My favorite sport or game is _____.

Activity 11

Unusual facts: _____

Rewrite A: _____

_____

_____

Rewrite B: _____

_____

_____

Activity 11A

Unusual facts: _____

Rewrite A: _____

_____

_____

Rewrite B: _____

_____

_____

Heighten Interest With Anecdotes

PURPOSE

to illustrate how to open a piece of writing with an anecdote. An anecdote is a brief story (four to six lines) that both introduces the content of your piece and sets the tone.

Before Example

Four-year-old Anthony had fun pretending and dreaming. He dreamed about flying. He dreamed of using his Batman cape and Donald Duck umbrella for flying.

Brainstorm Box

- rainy, boring day
- put on batman costume
- stood on railing—jumped
- climbed to 2nd floor
- opened Donald Duck umbrella

After Example

Four-year-old Anthony had always dreamed of flying. Now, dressed in his midnight blue Batman costume, Anthony rummaged through the hall closet until he found the Donald Duck umbrella. He climbed to the top of the stairs, opened the umbrella, balanced on the railing, and jumped. For a brief moment Anthony thought, I'm flying.

Get Students Involved

Ask: How does the anecdote affect the mood and tone? Why does it create interest? Why does the change in the verbs in the AFTER EXAMPLE improve this introduction? When is it effective to use an anecdote? Can you use this technique to open a nonfiction piece? [Yes; if you were writing a biography of the Wright brothers, for example, you might start with an anecdote about them designing and flying kites when they were young.] Can you find examples in your free-choice reading books to discuss during another class?

Directions: Choose one story idea, then brainstorm ideas and develop them into a short anecdote.

Activity 12

1 The the first time you are cooking dinner for your family and everything goes wrong.

2 You're alone in the house and hear strange noises in the basement.

3 During an all-day hike in the woods, you lose the group.

Brainstorm List: _____
_____
_____

Anecdote: _____
_____
_____
_____
_____
_____
_____

Activity 12A

1 Your next-door neighbor's pet snake escapes and is on your block.

2 Today is the day you are cutting your long hair.

3 You're locked in the bathroom, and nobody is home.

Brainstorm List: _____
_____
_____

Anecdote: _____
_____
_____
_____
_____
_____

Create You-Are-There Immediacy With Dialogue

PURPOSE

to show how inner thoughts or a revealing conversation between two characters can hook readers

Before Examples

1 Chico wasn't sure he wanted to visit his grandmother.

2 Jennell knew her father was a wet blanket, always saying "no" when she wanted to go out with her friends.

Brainstorm Box

- Chico loved his sick grandmother. Should he lie to his mom about visiting grandmother and go with his friends?

- Jennell wants to go to the mall without an adult. She plans to sneak out this time.

After Examples

1 Chico stood in front of the door wondering if he should open it. He thought about other visits when he sat in the dim room with his sick grandmother, wishing he was someplace else. Should he lie to his mom and skate with his friends instead of visiting his grandmother?

2 "I'll be at the mall with five other girls just for one hour. Please let me go, Dad. Maria's mom is driving us and picking us up," pleaded Jennell.

"You know the rule: no adult, no mall," said Mr. Rosario.
Jennell stomped up the stairs to her room. Minutes later, she slipped out the back door. I'll be gone one hour. He'll never miss me, she thought.

Get Students Involved

Ask: What do you learn from the inner thoughts and brief conversation? [unspoken feelings, reactions, plans, character traits] How did this improve the openings?

Directions: Choose one introduction and rewrite with inner thoughts and/or dialogue.

Activity 13

1 Rosa hated doing the dinner dishes. Tonight she'd find a way to convince her brother that it was his turn.

2 Mario was sick and tired of taking his little brother to the park every Saturday morning.

Rewrite: _____

_____

_____

_____

_____

_____

_____

Activity 13A

1 Judy worried about accepting the dare to race Paula, the best runner at their school.

2 The wallet Randy found had a twenty dollar bill inside and the name, address, and phone number of the woman who owned it. Randy wanted to keep it, but the wallet felt like a lump of lead in his hand.

Rewrite: _____

_____

_____

_____

_____

_____

_____

PART III

Create Strong Images With Figurative Language

Figurative language transmits ideas, sensations, and feelings intensely to others through arresting, apt images. Figurative language is to the writer what film and a camera are to the movie director. Like a director setting up a scene and choosing a camera angle, the writer uses figurative language to create a word picture that is laden with meaning.

The challenge facing writers who use figurative language is to invent new ways of describing feelings, things, and events—to paint fresh images with words. Figurative language helps readers visualize what you see and feel.

The mini-lessons in this section introduce five types of figurative language that can make students' writing sparkle.

Revision Tips

1 Reread your writing.

2 Place a check above a description that figurative language could improve. Choose one to three descriptions.

3 Circle figurative language that is ordinary, such as "quiet as a mouse." Instead of using everyday expressions, find or invent unusual ones.

4 Brainstorm a mini-list of unique ideas.

5 Choose the most effective idea and rewrite.

Compare With Similes

> **PURPOSE**
>
> to describe one thing by comparing it to something else; to show that two unlike things can be compared if they have one thing in common

Before Examples

1 The moon was thin.

2 There were lines of people at the football stadium.

3 The helicopter stayed in one place above the lighthouse.

Brainstorm Box

1 like: piece of string, rind of fruit, onion ring, silver hoop

2 like: cars on a bridge, a traffic jam, a line of ants

3 like: a fan's blades, a hummingbird

After Examples

1 The moon in the dark sky was as thin as a single onion ring.

2 Like cars in a traffic jam, the line of people inched its way toward the entrance to the football stadium.

3 The helicopter's blades spun like a hummingbird's wings as the aircraft hovered above the lighthouse.

Get Students Involved

Ask: How did the similes improve the images? What did the two things being compared have in common? Can you write other similes that are more effective?

Literary Examples

"With its silly neck a-bobbin' like a/ basket full o'snakes..."

—*Rudyard Kipling describing a camel.*

"Hilltops like hot iron glitter bright in the sun."

—*John Clare*

Directions: Before completing each activity, brainstorm ideas for similes.

Activity 14

Complete each sentence with a unique simile.

Brainstorm List:

1 My locker is as messy as _____

_____

2 His cold gaze was like _____

_____

3 Tears fell from her eyes like _____

_____

Activity 14 A

Choose two of the following items, then invent a simile for each and use it in a sentence.

1 a sneeze

Brainstorm List:

Sentence: _____

_____

2 cooked spaghetti

Brainstorm List:

Sentence: _____

_____

3 the stars

Brainstorm List:

Sentence: _____

_____

Use Metaphors to Create Memorable Pictures

PURPOSE

to show how to compare one thing to something else directly without using *like* or *as*; to experience the difference in emphasis between a simile and a metaphor

Before Examples

1 My toes are cold.
2 Leaves fall to the ground.
3 Her voice is loud when she gives orders.
4 The ball was tossed by the pitcher.

Brainstorm Box

1 snow, frost, ice cubes, icicles
2 snowflakes, dancers, seeds, gymnasts
3 fog horn, trumpet, drum
4 rocket, jet, eagle diving

After Examples

1 My toes are ice cubes.
2 Leaves are dancers, twirling to the ground.
3 Her voice is a trumpet blasting orders.
4 The zooming white comet sailed out of the pitcher's hand and across homeplate.

Get Students Involved

Ask: Why do you feel that readers might like metaphors? What is the difference between a metaphor and a simile? Is your image or understanding of the subject when described as a metaphor different than when it is described as a simile? How does it change? [Metaphor has no linking word; metaphor can have more impact, since two things are equated.]

Literary Examples

"The moon is a ghostly galleon, tossed on stormy seas."

—*Alfred Noyes*

"Rudolph Reed was oaken. His wife was oaken too."

—*Gwendolyn Brooks*

Directions: Brainstorm ideas before rewriting.

Activity 15

Choose two sentences and rewrite with a unique metaphor.

Brainstorm List:

1 The spy is creeping behind the building.

_____

2 The ballerina is graceful.

_____

3 Rows of telephone wires are along the street.

_____

Activity 15A

Choose two of the following things, invent a metaphor for each, and use it in a sentence.

1 the moon

Brainstorm List:

Sentence: _____

_____

2 school hallway

Brainstorm List:

Sentence: _____

_____

3 anger

Brainstorm List:

Sentence: _____

_____

Punch Up Writing With Personification

PURPOSE

to show that personification is a figure of speech that gives human qualities, such as speech, feelings, behavior, to something that doesn't have these qualities

Before Examples

1 The foghorn is sad.
2 The wind blew the leaves.
3 The ocean made me want to swim.
4 The moon goes in and out of the clouds.

Brainstorm Box

1 groan, moan, sigh, sings a dirge

2 worked hard, tried

3 beckoned, cried out, hollered, shouted, dared

4 plays tag, plays hide and seek, appears, disappears

After Examples

1 The foghorn moans with grief.
2 The wind tried and tried to scatter all the leaves.
3 The ocean shouted, daring me to swim.
4 The moon plays hide and seek in the clouds.

Get Students Involved

Ask: How does personification enhance your visual image of each sentence? Can you find different ways to personify the BEFORE EXAMPLES?

Directions: Brainstorm ideas before rewriting.

Activity 16

Use personification in your rewrites of two sentences. Feel free to change the sentence any way you wish. The words to personify are underlined.

Brainstorm List:

1 <u>Winter</u> makes frost designs on windowpanes.

_____

2 <u>Dewdrops</u> are on the grass in the morning.

_____

3 The <u>rusted old truck</u> went up the hill.

_____

Activity 16A

Choose two things to personify, and use each in a sentence.

1 the wind

Brainstorm List:

Sentence: _____

_____

2 a snake

Brainstorm List:

Sentence: _____

_____

3 the city

Brainstorm List:

Sentence: _____

_____

Oh, Onomatopoeia!

PURPOSE

to show how words that sound like what they mean enhance writing; to encourage students to invent original sound words

Before Examples

1 The wind blew.
2 The dive turned into a belly flop.
3 The demolition crew destroyed the building.

Brainstorm Box

1 whoosh, wheee   **2** splat, splash, splish

3 crash, bam, zing

After Examples

1 *Whooo!* went the wind, whirling leaves around the meadow.
2 Splat! The diver landed on her belly.
3 Bam! Bam! Bam! banged the steel ball, crumbling the building's wall.

Get Students Involved

Ask: How do the onomatopoeic words help you imagine the scene? [Sounds help create images; sounds appeal to senses; sounds can return you to a place; sounds reinforce and dramatize meaning.]

Literary Examples

"...Copper tong
brass clang
bronze bong,

The bell gives
Metal a tongue..."

—Valerie Worth

Activity 17

Think of an onomatopoeic word or short phrase to describe the sound each item below can make. Try making up original sound words.

ITEM   ONOMATOPOEIC WORD

1 breaking glass   **1** _____

2 chewing ice cubes   **2** _____

3 rain-filled sneakers   **3** _____
   on a walking student

4 trudging through mud   **4** _____

Activity 17A

Choose three of the four completed items above. Use each with its onomatopoeic word or phrase in a complete sentence.

1 _____

_____

_____

2 _____

_____

_____

3 _____

_____

_____

Spice Up Your Writing With Synesthesia

Mini-Lesson 18

PURPOSE

to show how to enhance images by mingling the senses of sight, sound, taste, smell, and touch (sight mixes with sound, taste mixes with touch, etc.)

Before Examples

1 After learning about the fatal crash, angry thoughts filled his mind.
2 The velvet pillow felt soft, soothing her headache.
3 The upholstery was bright.
4 The music was smooth.

Brainstorm Box

1 gray, black, ocher, waves, pound

2 purple, blue, topaz, quiet, hush

3 neon, loud, bright

4 light, silvery, breezy, smooth pudding

After Examples

1 After learning about the fatal crash, black images sounded like pounding waves.
2 The light blue hush of the plush velvet pillow soothed her headache.
3 The psychedelic zebra-stripe pattern on the sofa was so loud, Al couldn't hear Jimmy speaking.
4 The silvery tones of her flute tasted like smooth custard.

Get Students Involved

Ask: How do the mixed sensations strengthen your image of the subject or your understanding of the experience?

Literary Examples

"To the bugle, every color is red."

—*Emily Dickinson*

"The taste of marshmallows sounds like the sea in a shell."

—*Anina Robb*

Activity 18

Write a short poem using a mixture of at least two senses: sight, smell, hearing, taste, touch

Sample Poem: the moon's
                  silver talk misted
                  the meadow
                  in a peppermint glow

Brainstorm List: _____

_____

_____

_____

Activity 18A

Rewrite two of the three sentences using synesthesia.

1 She whispered fearful thoughts to herself.

2 The smell of cookies aroused hunger.

3 We lay in the snow.

Rewrite 1: _____

_____

_____

_____

Rewrite 2: _____

_____

_____

_____

More Fun Writing Challenges

Use these writing challenges after students have completed the activities and improved their writing. Place a challenge on the chalkboard and give students ten minutes to finish a first draft. Have students complete a mini-brainstorm before writing. Remind them of their arsenal of techniques and that their goal is to write exciting, engaging sentences.

1 In two sentences set the scene in a school bus, school cafeteria, on a soccer field, or in the supermarket.

2 Describe one of these smells: your favorite cake; pizza; a barn with pigs, horses, or cows.

3 In two or three sentences, create a word picture of your room, the breakfast table, the beach, or fishing at a pond.

4 Use words to create a picture of an elderly person with a limp, crossing the street.

5 Write the inner thoughts of a runner (or any other athlete) just before the most important event or game of the year.

6 Write a short diary entry about an important moment in your life.

7 Use the five senses (sight, hearing, smell, touch, taste) to describe your favorite place to be away from school.

8 Write a stream of consciousness piece. For ten minutes jot down everything that comes to mind. Include what you think, feel, and sense during this time.

9 Describe a smell that you dislike intensely. Can you compare it to something? How does it make you feel? What does it make you think?

10 Free write for ten minutes. Write continuously without lifting your pen about any ideas that come to mind. To keep ideas flowing, you might have to write a word again and again until you get another idea.

11 In two or three sentences, describe the worst meal you've ever eaten.

12 Write your inner thoughts as you prepare to try out for the cheerleading squad, a team, an orchestra, or a part in a play.

13 Show with words what your best friend's face looks like.

14 Think of a person you admire, and in a sentence or two tell why.

15 Describe a baby taking its first steps.

16 Use words to help us see a dog chasing a cat or squirrel.

17 In two to three sentences, re-create your favorite season.

18 Use figurative language to describe a deserted house you've entered.

19 Describe the happiest, saddest, or most frightening experience of your life.

20 If you could travel anyplace in the universe, where would you go and why?

21 Write directions, in proper sequence, for one of the following: making a turkey sandwich, setting the table for dinner, or playing one of your favorite games.

22 Create a commercial for your favorite product.

23 Write a short piece trying to persaude your mom or dad to let you have a pet.

24 In two or three sentences, describe your favorite place to be at school.

25 Use synesthesia to describe your reaction to winning a major sports event, a writing contest, or the science fair.